L•LEONARD
STRUMENTAL
PLAY-ALONG

AUDIO
ACCESS
INCLUDED

AYBACK+
Pitch • Balance • Loop

OBOE

STAR WARS

MUSIC FROM AL[...]S

T0085213

2 Across the Stars (Love Theme from "*Star Wars: Attack of the Clones*")
3 Ahch-To Island
4 Battle of the Heroes
6 Cantina Band
8 Duel of the Fates
10 The Forest Battle
12 Han Solo and the Princess
13 The Imperial March (Darth Vader's Theme)
14 March of the Resistance
16 May the Force Be with You
18 Princess Leia's Theme
20 Rey's Theme
17 The Rise of Skywalker
22 Star Wars (Main Theme)
23 Throne Room *and* End Title
24 Yoda's Theme

Audio arrangements by Peter Deneff

To access audio, visit:
www.halleonard.com/mylibrary

"Enter Code"
4636-9913-2637-8111

ISBN 978-1-70510-719-5

HAL•LEONARD®

Visit Hal Leonard Online at
www.halleonard.com

Contact us:
Hal Leonard
7777 West Bluemound Road
Milwaukee, WI 53213
Email: info@halleonard.com

In Europe, contact:
Hal Leonard Europe Limited
42 Wigmore Street
Marylebone, London, W1U 2RN
Email: info@halleonardeurope.com

In Australia, contact:
Hal Leonard Australia Pty. Ltd.
4 Lentara Court
Cheltenham, Victoria, 3192 Australia
Email: info@halleonard.com.au

ACROSS THE STARS

(Love Theme from *"STAR WARS: ATTACK OF THE CLONES"*)

OBOE

Music by JOHN WILLIAM

AHCH-TO ISLAND

from *STAR WARS: THE LAST JEDI*

OBOE

Music by JOHN WILLIAMS

BATTLE OF THE HEROES

from *STAR WARS: REVENGE OF THE SITH*

OBOE

By JOHN WILLIAM

2
2
3
4
ff

CANTINA BAND

from *STAR WARS: A NEW HOPE*

OBOE

Music by JOHN WILLIAM

D.S. al Coda
CODA

DUEL OF THE FATES

from *STAR WARS: THE PHANTOM MENACE*

OBOE

Music by JOHN WILLIAM

4
f
6
mp
mf
f
3
3
ff

THE FOREST BATTLE

from *STAR WARS: RETURN OF THE JEDI*

OBOE

Music by JOHN WILLIAM

2
2
mf
4
4
f
mf

HAN SOLO AND THE PRINCESS

from *STAR WARS: THE EMPIRE STRIKES BACK*

OBOE

Music by JOHN WILLIAMS

THE IMPERIAL MARCH

(Darth Vader's Theme)

from *STAR WARS: THE EMPIRE STRIKES BACK*

OBOE

Music by JOHN WILLIAMS

MARCH OF THE RESISTANCE

from *STAR WARS: THE FORCE AWAKENS*

OBOE

Music by JOHN WILLIAMS

3
mf
mp
mf
f
f
ff
fff

MAY THE FORCE BE WITH YOU

from *STAR WARS: A NEW HOPE*

OBOE

Music by JOHN WILLIAMS

THE RISE OF SKYWALKER

from *STAR WARS: THE RISE OF SKYWALKER*

OBOE

Composed by JOHN WILLIAMS

PRINCESS LEIA'S THEME

from *STAR WARS: A NEW HOPE*

OBOE

Music by JOHN WILLIAM

f
rit.
p

REY'S THEME

from *STAR WARS: THE FORCE AWAKENS*

OBOE

Music by JOHN WILLIAMS

mf
Broadly
f
ff
rit.
Tempo I
mp
p
rit.
pp

STAR WARS
(Main Theme)
from *STAR WARS: A NEW HOPE*

OBOE

Music by JOHN WILLIAM

THRONE ROOM *and* END TITLE

from *STAR WARS: A NEW HOPE*

OBOE

Music by JOHN WILLIAMS

YODA'S THEME

from *STAR WARS: THE EMPIRE STRIKES BACK*

OBOE

Music by JOHN WILLIAM